HANGIN' LOOSE!

A Kid's Guide To Oahu, Hawaii

Bellissima Publishing, LLC
Jamul, California
www.bellissimapublishing.com

copyright © 2009 by Penny D. Weigand & John D. Weigand

All rights reserved. No part of this book may be reproduced or transmitted in any form or by any means, electronic or mechanical, including photocopying, recording, or by any other means, or by any information or storage retrieval system, without permission from the publisher.

ISBN 1-935118-78-1
First Edition

Acknowledgements

A special thanks and acknowledgment to:

The Honolulu Cookie Company & to model Hyunhee Yuk

Aoki's Shave Ice where four generations have served shave ice on the North Shore since 1931

The Pearl Factory, Hawaii's original Pearl In The Oyster

To the Hawaiian People and to "The Spirit Of Aloha"

Hangin' Loose!

Bellissima Publishing, LLC

Introduction

Ohau, Hawaii is a great place to visit! Walk the beach of Waikiki, swim in the ocean, see a movie on the beach! You can do it all. 'Hangin' Loose' is the style, so put yourself on Hawaiian time and have fun in the sun!

This is a new kind of picture book for kids, a kid's special guide to a very special place, and like all the Penelope Dyan and John D. Weigand collaborations, a book meant for kids that will look great on your coffee table. Told in the simplest form and in a fun way, Dyan sees with the eyes of a child; and she will introduce you to a myriad of things to do when you are in Oahu in a very noncommercial way. (That is, it will not cost an arm and a leg to please the children and have some real family fun when on vacation.)

Anyone can do a book about the ordinary, the tourist traps, a boring book filled with places and facts. This is a book filled with the spirit of Aloha, a book you do not want to miss. Enjoy the simple (written for kids) poetry of award winning author, Penelope Dyan, and the beautiful color photographs of John D. Weigand. Find out what fun really is and see the real Oahu, Hawaii! Mahalo!

Hangin' Loose!

Bellissima Publishing, LLC

Hangin' Loose!

A Kid's Guide To Oahu, Hawaii

Photography By John D. Weigand
Poetry by Penelope Dyan

If you go to Oahu you can have a ball. . .
If you go to Oahu you can do it all. . .
You can go surfing. . .

You can swim at the beach...

You can have treats, see a movie,

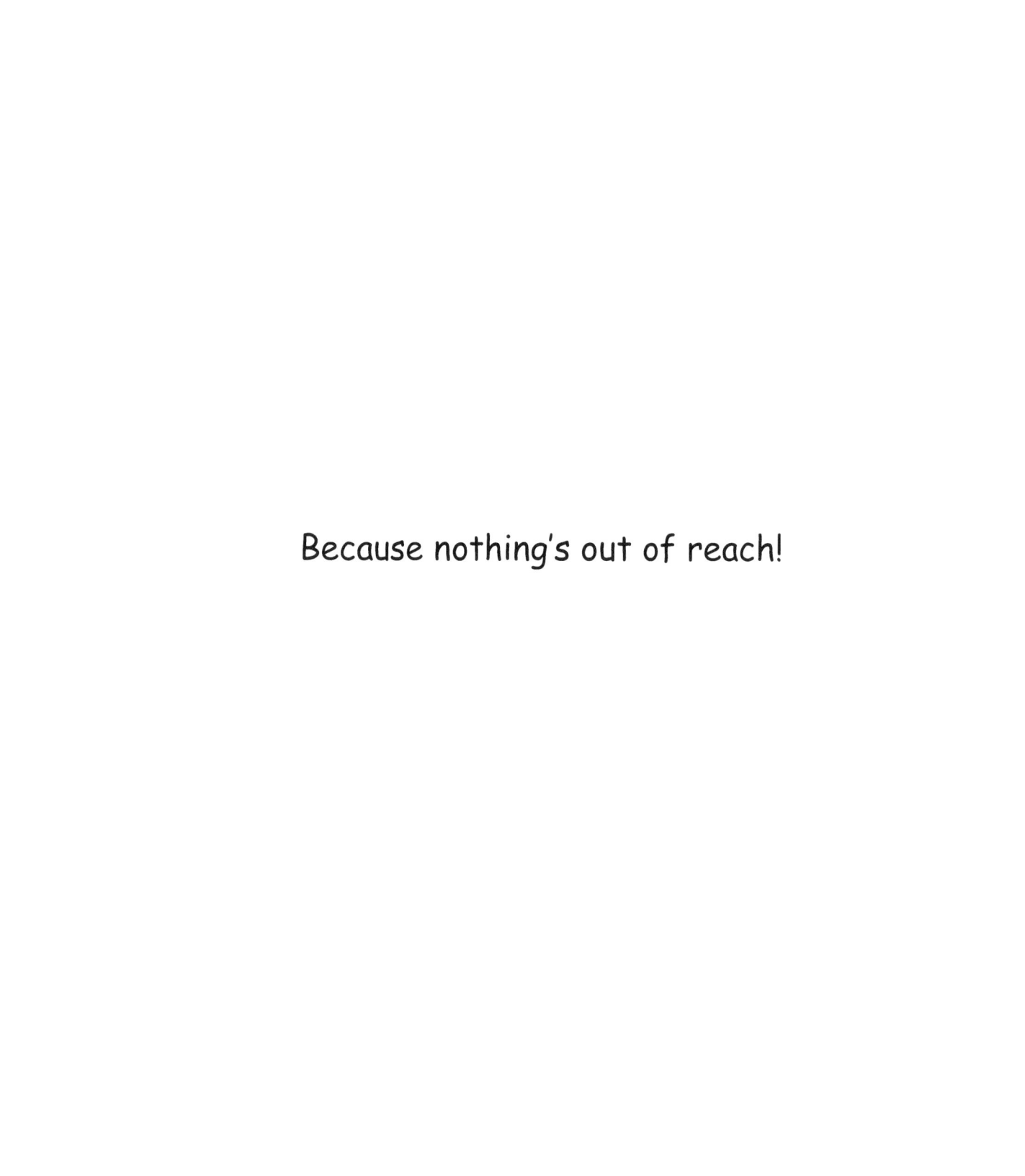

Because nothing's out of reach!

You can get a pearl from an oyster's shell...

Buy cookies from a place I know REALLY well.
(There are loads of samples there you can eat,
BEFORE you choose your special treat!)

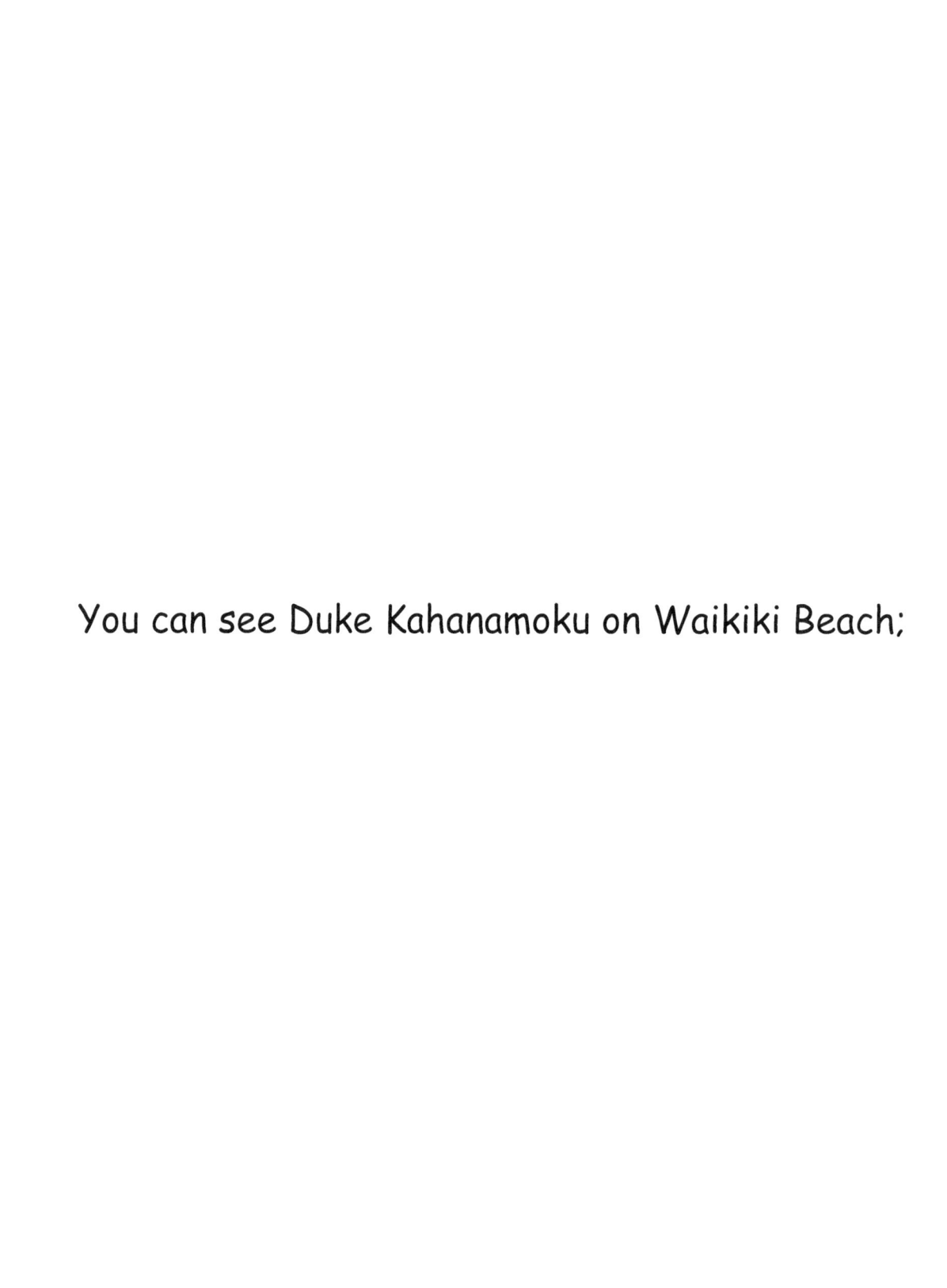

You can see Duke Kahanamoku on Waikiki Beach;

And King Kamehameha with his royal arm outreached.

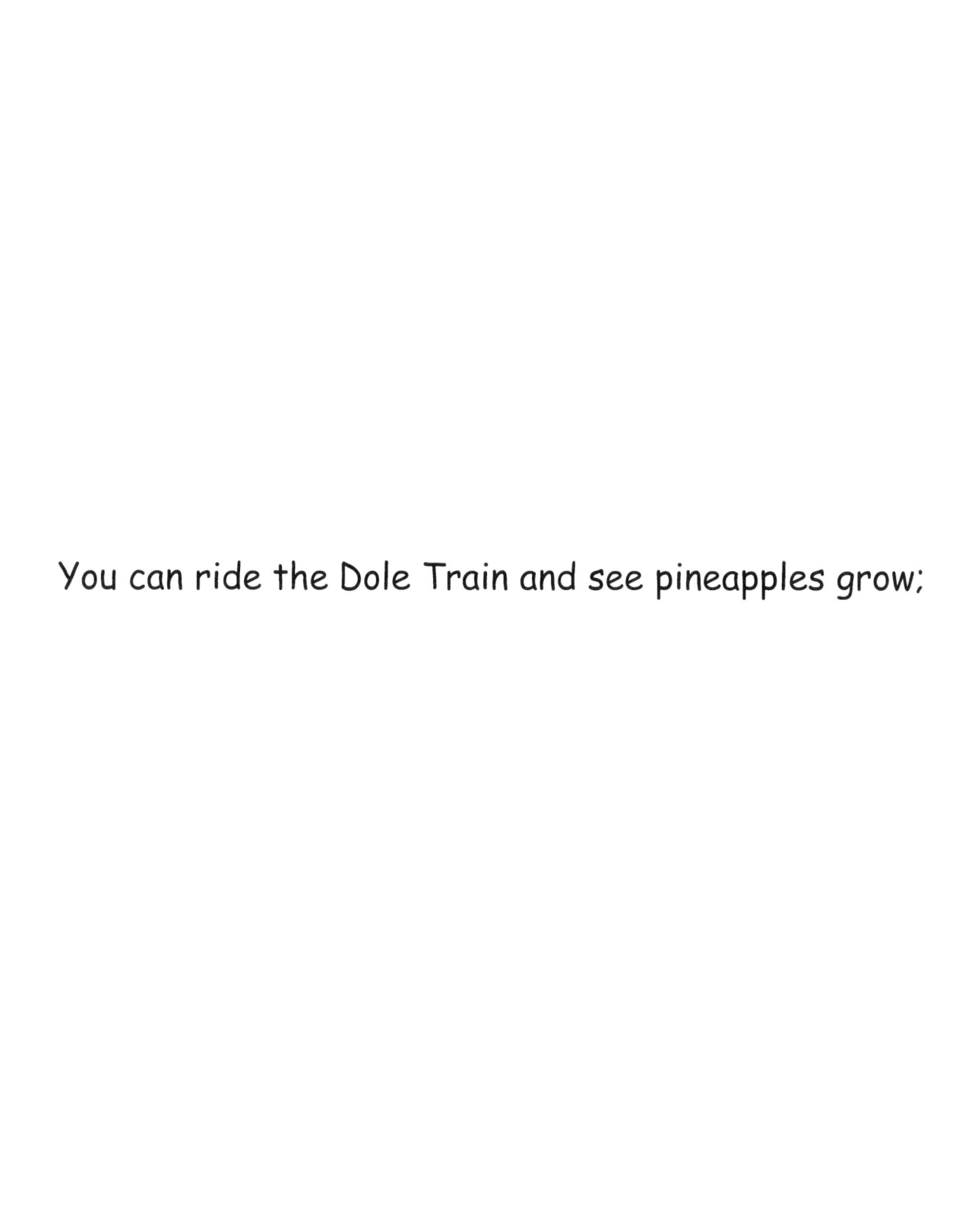

You can ride the Dole Train and see pineapples grow;

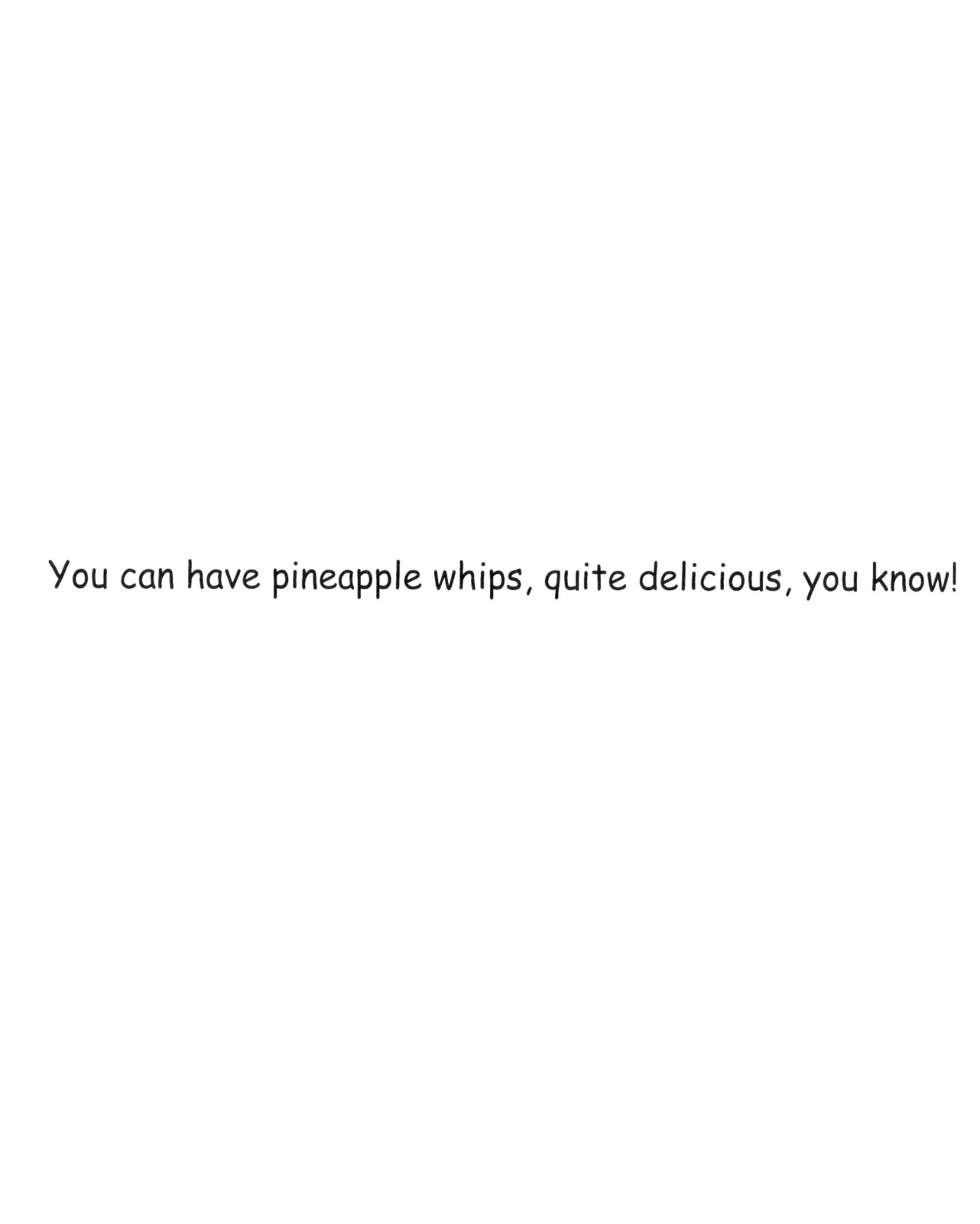

You can have pineapple whips, quite delicious, you know!

You can go to a swap meet and have some more fun,
On Saturdays and Sundays 'till with shopping you're done.

And when you're hot and thirsty drive to North Shore...

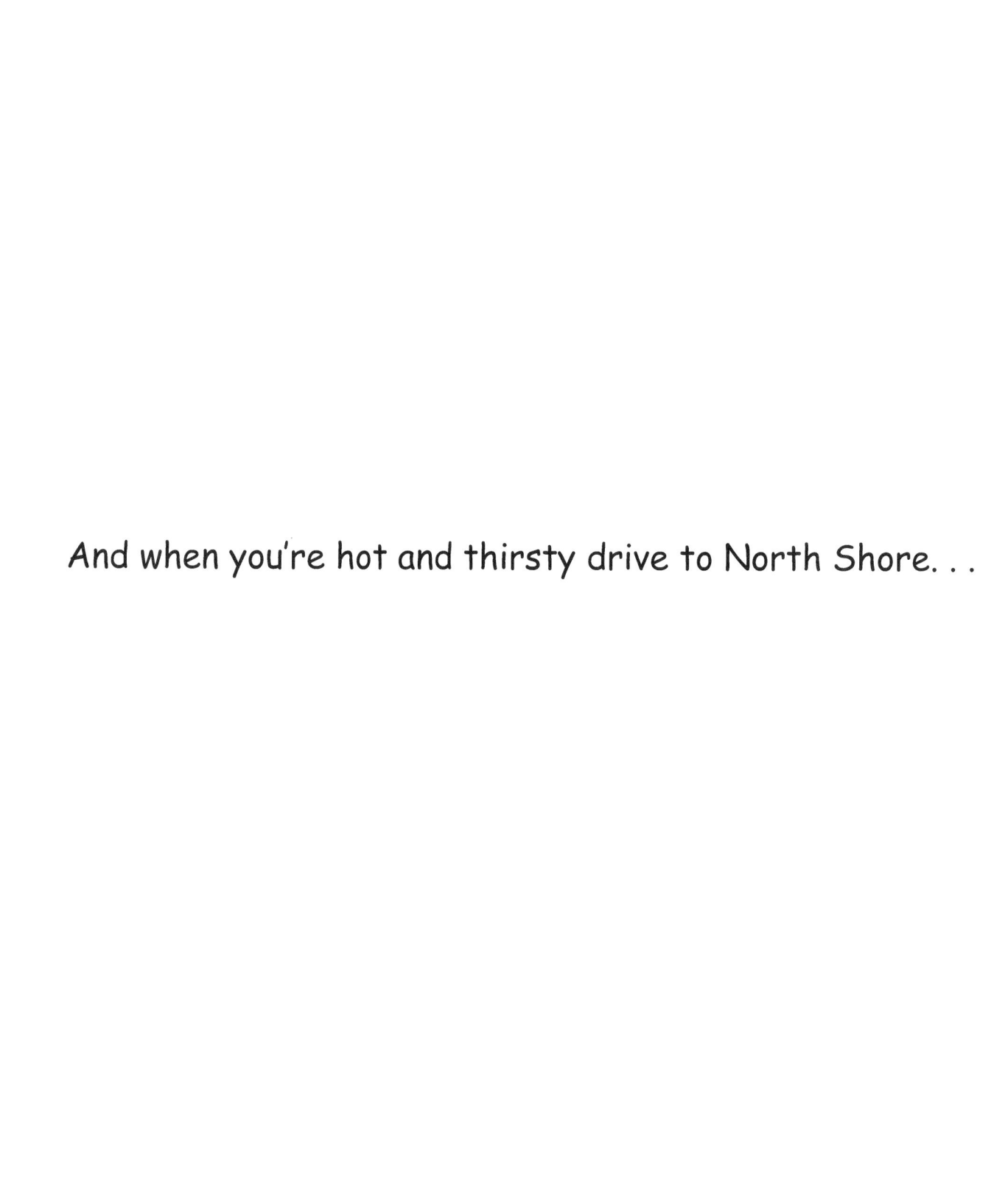

Where you can buy shave ice and oh so much more!

Above Hanauma Bay you can also see
A mongoose playing by a tree.

You can swim, snorkel, see colorful fish. . .

See a sunset, if you wish.
In Ohau, Hawaii there's a lot you can do;
Because Hawaii's for everyone, even keiki's like you!

So into the sunset do take a sail,
Swim, snorkel or see a whale!
Because you NEVER know what YOU will see,
When you go for a sail on Waikiki!
And since "Aloha" means both hello and goodbye,
When it's time to go home, there's no need to cry;
Because to Hawaii you'll come again,
It's just a matter of where and when.

Aloha Means
Never having to Say Goodbye!

www.ingramcontent.com/pod-product-compliance
Ingram Content Group UK Ltd.
Pitfield, Milton Keynes, MK11 3LW, UK
UKHW060137240426
12048UKWH00002B/76